SABRINA COLON

From Rock Bottom to Rich Energy

For every woman who's ever been broke, broken, or overlooked- this is your comeback manual.

Dedication
This one is for me.
For the woman who survived it all.
Who kept going when no one clapped.
Who rebuilt herself brick by brick.
Who dared to dream, then made it happen.
I did this. And I'm damn proud of it.

Contents

Acknowledgments

To God —

You carried me through the fire. You answered prayers I whispered in the dark. You gave me the strength to rise when I thought I couldn't. This book is proof of Your power. Thank You for never leaving my side.

To my children, Sahara and King —

You are my why. You are the light in every room and the love that fuels my purpose. Watching you grow is my greatest joy, and I pray this book plants seeds of strength and wealth in your hearts.

To my bonus daughter Tiara —

Thank you for loving me like your own, for being there through every moment of healing, and for loving your little brother with a heart so full it humbles me. Your presence is one of the greatest gifts in our lives.

To My Family —

Thank you for shaping parts of this journey, both seen and unseen.

To Shane —

Thank you for being the kind of sister-friend who sees the dream before it's fully formed, and for walking beside me with love, laughter, and steadfast belief.

iv

To Aisha —

Your joy for me never felt fake. You clap loud, love hard, and I'm so grateful for your unwavering light.

To Mimi —

For guiding me with discernment, for sending me my bible verses, and lifting me up with encouragement every single day. Your love has covered me.

To Brianna —

For keeping me sane when the job made me crazy. You are truly appreciated!

To Brandi —

You're the real MVP! Thank you for helping me craft my thoughts and joining me on this journey, I truly couldn't have done this without you!

And finally...

To every woman who's ever doubted herself, dimmed her light, or felt like she had to start over — this book was written for you. I see you. I *am* you. And I promise you, the glow-up is **real.**

Prologue

Dear Reader,

This book was born from the trenches.

Not from a six-figure coaching program or a glossy, highlight-reel life—but from real struggle, real loss, real grit. I wrote this for the person who has been counted out, who has counted themselves out, and who is ready to take that power back.

I've made big money moves—and big money mistakes. I've cried in my car, lost everything, rebuilt, and found myself in rooms I used to only dream about. If you're here, I want you to know something: you're not broken, you're just stuck in survival—and this book is your permission slip to move beyond that.

You won't find fluff or generic advice here. You'll find real-life lessons, raw stories, and a step-by-step glow-up plan rooted in experience, not perfection. I don't have all the answers, but I do have receipts—and the roadmap I used to get from rock bottom to rich energy.

Let's be clear: this isn't just a money book.

It's a mindset shift. A healing journey. A declaration that your past does not get to have the final say.

I'm honored to walk this road with you.

Let's glow up—for real this time.

With love and truth,

Sabrina Colón

1

You're Not Broken- You're Just Stuck in Survival

Let me tell you something I wish someone had told me a long time ago:

You are not broken.
  You're not lazy.
  You're not irresponsible.
  You're not a lost cause.
  You are simply a human being who has been in survival mode for so long, you forgot what it
  feels like to breathe.
  We don't talk about survival mode enough.
  We glamorize hustle, glorify the grind, and tell people to keep pushing—but nobody asks
  why you're so tired, or *how* you've been expected to carry it all without a breakdown.
  Maybe you're juggling a job that drains you, bills that suffo-cate you, and responsibilities

that feel like anchors.

You're raising kids while trying to raise yourself.

You're managing chronic illness while still showing up for everybody else.

You're fighting invisible battles while people wonder why you don't smile more.

And the worst part? You've internalized it.

You've looked at your messy kitchen, your bank account, your unfinished to-do list and

whispered to yourself,

"What's wrong with me?"

But I'm here to answer that for you.

Nothing.

There is nothing wrong with you.

You've been operating in fight, flight, or freeze—just trying to stay afloat.

You were surviving on scraps of time, energy, and sometimes love.

And when your nervous system is locked in survival mode, it's not thinking about meal

prep or Roth IRAs or vision boards.

It's thinking: *how do I make it through the day?*

So let's get this straight right now:

This book isn't about shaming your past.

This isn't about financial perfection or emotional tidiness.

This is about reclaiming your power.This is your pivot.

Because the truth is—your glow-up doesn't start when everything is perfect.

It starts when you say:

"I'm done surviving. I'm ready to build something different."

That doesn't mean the bills stop.

That doesn't mean the healing is over.

But it does mean that from this moment forward, we're shifting.

From reactive to intentional.

From just existing... to designing the life you deserve.

You're not behind.

You're not too late.

You're right on time for your next chapter.

So take a breath.

Shake off the shame.

And keep reading—because baby, this book is your mirror and your blueprint.

You're not broken. You're rebuilding.

One page at a time.

One step at a time.

One glow-up at a time. ♥

2

The "Oh Hell No" Moment

I had just closed my very first home sale to my cousin Luis and his wife Lola when they

referred me to Lola's sister, Jessica. Jessica and her husband were looking to buy, and I was
ready to show up like a professional.
There was only one problem—I didn't have a car.
Not a decent one anyway.
At the time, I was flat broke, still trying to crawl out of debt, and had no money for a vehicle.
So I was borrowing my parents' old, beat-up Nissan Sentra just to get around. That car had
so many issues. Every time we stopped to see a house, I'd have to ask Jessica to "go ahead
and try it," then I'd pop the hood, pull out a hammer, and tap the starter like a mechanic in
heels.
I'd yell, "Try it!" and off we'd go—house to house, praying

the damn thing wouldn't

fall apart.

One day, I ran out of gas with Jessica in the car.

Ran. Out. Of. Gas.

Her husband had to come bring us a gas can, and I was *mortified.*

I told her, "Jessica, you can fire me right now, I get it. I'm so sorry."

And do you know what she said?

"I'm not going to fire you, Sabrina."

She didn't.

She and her husband bought a house with me.

They believed in me even when my circumstances didn't look like much.

I'll never forget that.

At that point, I was also a full-time mom. I had my baby in the back seat in a car seat while

showing homes, doing everything I could to hold it together, grinding from a place of pure

will.

And in the middle of all the chaos, there were still little moments of joy.

Like one time when I thought I saw a friend while driving and started waving like

crazy—only to realize it was not who I thought it was.

Jessica and I were crying laughing in the car.

We had the best time house hunting, even with all the chaos.

And you know what?

That month ended up being a **game-changer**.

After Jessica closed on her house, my cousin Maria referred her friends Fernando and

Teresa.The very first house I showed them is the one they bought.

That month, I made **$27,000**.

Before taxes, sure—but it was the most money I had ever made in my life.

I paid off about $10,000 in debt (even though I didn't know at the time I could've disputed

some of it).

I took $4,500 and bought a car from an auction—a burgundy Mazda with a big dent on the

side.

You couldn't even test drive it before buying. You just started the engine, listened, and

hoped for the best.

And guess what?

It ran.

And so did I.

I ran straight out of survival mode and into my first glow-up.

No, it wasn't easy.

Yes, it was exhausting.

But I proved something to myself in that moment.

Even when I was dead broke, in debt, embarrassed, and hustling in a junk car—I was still

out here selling homes, showing up, and making moves.

That was my **'Oh Hell No'** moment.

The moment I realized:

"I will never again allow someone else to control my life— financially or

otherwise. I will build it myself."

That was the day I knew:

I might not have had it all figured out, but I had fire.

And that fire?
Got me free.

💡 **Glow-Up Takeaway:**

● Your circumstances don't define your potential—**your persistence does.**

● You don't need the "perfect setup" to start winning—you just need to start.

● Don't let where you are keep you from believing in where you're going.

● Sometimes, the glow-up starts in a car that needs a hammer and prayer.

3

The Mercedes Mistake- When My Dream Car Became a Financial Nightmare

When I was about 30 years old, after selling a few homes and finally getting myself out of

debt, I decided it was time for an upgrade. I'd been driving a burgundy Mazda I bought at

an auction—complete with a huge dent in the side. It got the job done, but I was starting to

feel like, *If I really want to make an impression on my clients, I need to show up*

differently. I wanted a newer, nicer car. Something that looked the part.

One day, I was driving down the highway and saw the cutest car. I mean it—I *gasped.* It was

love at first sight! I had to know what it was. I sped up, pulled up next to it, and saw the badge: **a Mercedes.**

Ugh. I thought, *Yeah right. I could never afford one of those.*

Well, I was seeing this guy named Steve at the time, and he invited me to go look at cars

with him. I figured, why not? So off we went.

Straight to the Mercedes dealership.

He already knew exactly what he wanted. But as I walked the lot with him, I noticed

something surprising—some of those beautiful cars were actually **within my price range.**

My heart started racing.

I wanted one.

But I was scared. Real estate doesn't offer guaranteed pay-checks, and I didn't know if I

could afford the responsibility.

Then Steve turned to me and said:

"Go ahead and buy the car. I've got a listing for you."

Just like that.

That was all the permission I needed.

I walked back to the salesman, told him I wanted **leather seats**, a **sunroof**, a **navigation**

system (this was *a long time ago*—so that was high-tech at the time), **under 50k miles,**

and a sticker price of **under $25,000.**

He searched the whole lot, and eventually came back and said, "There's only one that meets

all your specs."

And *honey*, when I saw her? She was **perfect.**

A white Mercedes-Benz C240 with tan interior.

She had everything I asked for. She was *gorgeous.* I was ready.

My credit was okay—not established, but no collections. The

salesman couldn't finalize the

deal that day, but he said he'd work on it and get back to me.A few days later, I got the call:

"Come pick up your car."

I pulled $5,000 from my savings and walked into that dealership with a cashier's check in

hand. I was glowing.

When I drove off that lot, I felt like I was in a movie. I looked around at the other cars on

the freeway like:

"Look at me. I'm one of them now. I'm the one people admire."

I was living the dream.

Until the dream turned into a damn nightmare.

The first time I took the car in for service, I can't even remember what it needed—but I *do*

remember the price:

$1,000.

I was shocked.

And that was just the beginning.

Every time I brought it in—for brakes, for maintenance, for *anything*—it was another

$1,000. And another. And another.

Brakes on a Mercedes?

Baby, that's not just pads. That's **rotors.** Full replacements. Specialty parts.

It was a money pit.

And I was not financially prepared for the upkeep.

Now?

I drive a **Honda Accord.**

And the first time I took it in for service and they told me it would be **$60**, I nearly

screamed.

I've never been so thrilled in my life.

Looking back now, I can't help but laugh.

Why was I so damn foolish?

You live and you learn, I guess.

But if I could go back and talk to my younger self, I'd tell her one thing:

"Practicality is the real flex."

More money in your pocket means more money to **invest**, to **build**, to **breathe**.

I threw so much money into that Mercedes, I'm embarrassed.

But you know what?

That was part of the lesson.

💡 ***Glow-Up Reminder:***

● The real dream isn't the luxury car. It's financial peace.

● Flexing too early can cost you years of progress.

● Make sure your money can maintain the image you're chasing—or don't chase it at all.

4

The $50K Loss- When Love Cost Me Everything (But Not My Power)

I thought I had met my soulmate.

After a year and a half of picking up the pieces from a heartbreak that shattered me, I finally
opened myself up again. And there he was—charming, smart, handsome. He said all the
right things. He told me everything I wanted to hear. He made me feel wanted, seen, and
safe. He said he wanted a child with me. At first, I thought he was crazy... but eventually, I
said yes.
And then I became a mother for the second time.
During that time, the pandemic hit. Life shifted. The world shut down. And I was doing
everything I could to keep myself and my son afloat. He was in North Carolina, I was in
California. He told me he was getting his commercial driver's

license and had an

opportunity to become an over-the-road truck driver—but he needed help. He said if I could

just help him buy a truck, he'd move to California immediately. We'd get married, raise our

son together, and finally become a family.

"As soon as you send the money, I'm coming."

I believed him. I wanted the dream so badly. So I dipped into my retirement

account—something I never imagined doing. But during the pandemic, the rules were

relaxed. People were pulling out money to buy homes, invest, or stay afloat.

I thought I was investing in my future.

I thought I was investing in love.

I withdrew **$50,000**, set aside $5K for taxes, and sent him **$45,000.**

And then... nothing.

He didn't buy the truck.

He didn't move.

He didn't keep his word.

He conned me.

Eventually, he came to stay with us for about six months. He got a job with a trucking

company but things weren't working out the way I was expecting— especially as I began

feeling unwell. I was sleeping more, fatigued all the time, but I didn't yet know that my body

was breaking down.

And when I needed support the most... he left.The heartbreak was unbearable—but what made it worse was that I **held onto**

hope for

four more years. I kept believing that maybe he'd turn around. Maybe he'd pay me back.

Maybe he'd finally show up.

He didn't.

And what hurts the most? I never got that money back. Not a dime.

But what I *did* get was a fire in my soul that couldn't be put out.

That season of my life was *one of the hardest I've ever lived through.*

In February 2022, I was already declining. I kept showing up to work, telling my boss I

didn't feel well, but I couldn't explain it. She finally looked me in the eyes and said,

"Sabrina, you're sick."

And that's when I finally called the doctor.

I was scheduled to leave for Hawaii the next day. It was supposed to be a beautiful,

memory-making trip with my son. I didn't have time to get tests done before I left, so I

thought, *Maybe I'll feel better in paradise.*

But when I got there—I was so sick. So weak. I spent most of the trip in bed, forcing myself

out just to give my son one last joyful memory. At one point, I got a strange rash all over my

legs—tiny red dots. Another day, I felt like I was going to throw up by the pool. My friend

handed me a pain pill to help me get through it. I was pushing through that trip thinking...

What if this is it?

What if I don't come back from this?

But something else happened in Hawaii too.

Something *unexplainable.*

My Facebook exploded.

Out of nowhere, I got **3,000 friend requests in a single day.** My followers multiplied

overnight. I had been sharing little moments of my life, my son, my heart... but suddenly,

people were paying attention. Something was happening.

I knew in that moment—I had to *do something* with this.

Just one month earlier, after our whole house had gotten COVID, the seed for **Latinas on**

Wall Street had been planted. That vision came to me *in the middle of crisis.* And while I

was in bed recovering from both illness and heartbreak... I started building. I kept creating.

I kept believing there was more for me—even if I had to build it one exhausted breath at a

time.When I got home from Hawaii, I returned to work for *half a day* and ended up in the ER.

That was the beginning of **five months in bed**, which eventually led to my diagnosis:

lupus.

But here's what nobody tells you:

Sometimes your glow-up begins *in the darkness.*

While I was bedridden, I studied for a transportation supervisor position—something that

would nearly double my income. When I got the email to test, I could barely walk. But I

went. I passed.

Then came the interviews.

17

I was so weak I could hardly sit upright, but I pushed through, because I had something to

prove—not to them, but to myself. What no one saw was that I had prayed—*hard*. I begged

God to help me. To give me *just one* shot to get out of that bed, to feel like myself again. And

I know it was Him who carried me.

Because when I sat down for those interviews, it was like something came over me.

Every single question they asked? I had studied it. Drilled it. Prepared for it like I was

training for war. And when I answered, it was as if the words flowed through me. I felt like

Neo in *The Matrix*. I wasn't guessing—**I *knew*. I *felt* it.**

In September 2022, I got the job.

And with it came the confirmation:

He might have taken my money.

He might have broken my heart.

But he didn't take my future.

God made sure of that.

5

I'm That Girl

(Summer 2021 — Before the Diagnosis, Before the Title, But Deep in the Becoming)

There's a moment in every woman's story where she stops waiting to be chosen—and
  chooses herself.
  Mine happened in the summer of 2021.
  At the time, I was still a transportation clerk. I was showing up to work every day, doing my
  job, managing my household, and feeling... off. My body was starting to send warning signs,
  but I didn't know yet how serious it was. I hadn't been diagnosed. I hadn't hit any of the
  milestones that would come later. But something inside me was **shifting**.
  And then, one ordinary afternoon, I was scrolling through my phone—mind tired, soul
  restless—and this influencer popped up. He was from the

hood, just like me. And he was

confidently giving out financial advice—talking stocks, savings, credit, all the basics of

financial literacy.

And I sat there watching him, thinking...

"Hold up... I know all this. I've been living this. I've read the books,

made the mistakes, cleaned up my credit, built my retirement. I've

lived this ten times over."

And that's when the voice came in—clear, loud, and from deep inside:

"I could do this. I *should* be doing this. I'm not just somebody with a

story—I'm somebody with a blueprint."

But here I was... hiding.

Still doubting myself.

Still telling myself maybe I wasn't ready.

Still feeling like someone else would always be more polished, more perfect, more...

something.

So I called one of my best friends, Aisha.

I told her everything.

I said, "There are people out there who probably know more than me. Who've done more. I

don't know if I can really put myself out there like this."

She didn't hesitate."Sabrina," she said, "there *might* be people who know more than you. But are

they doing it?"

"The people who are doing it... are the people who are doing it."

20

Whew.

That line cracked something open in me.

Because that influencer? He wasn't more educated. He wasn't more brilliant.

He was just **bold.** He was out there. He was doing it.

And I wasn't anymore willing to sit in the shadows of people who were just willing to try.

So I did it.

I pulled out my phone, and I made my first video.

And girl... I was **scared.**

My heart was racing. My hands were sweating.

I hated the sound of my voice. I nitpicked everything—my appearance, my tone, my

lighting, my background.

But I did it anyway.

And I posted it.

That first video? **Thousands of views.** Just like that.

People were commenting, engaging, sharing.

And I realized something I'll never forget:

They weren't waiting for me to be perfect.

They were just waiting for me to *show up.*

That summer, I made a few more videos. Some took off. Some didn't.

But I was building something real.

Then life took a turn—I got sicker.

The full five-month spiral into my lupus diagnosis hadn't started yet, but the signs were

coming.

Eventually, I had to pause everything.

Focus on healing. Focus on surviving.

But by then, the seed was planted.

The voice was unlocked.

And even though I wasn't a transportation supervisor yet, even though I didn't have big

money or a big platform, I knew:I *was* that girl.

Not because I was on top of the world.

But because I had already decided **to rise no matter what.**

💡 **Glow-Up Takeaway:**

● Sometimes the realization comes *before* the reward.

● You don't need to be at your peak to know your power.

● You don't have to be the loudest, smartest, or flashiest—just the one who *starts*.

● And as Aisha said:

"The people who are doing it... are the people who are doing it."

● You don't need the whole staircase. You just need to take the first damn step.

6

The Foreclosure & The Foolery

Sometimes the biggest financial losses don't come from bad deals or bad luck.

They come from *bad partnerships*—especially the ones you tried to *rescue* instead of
   release.
   This chapter?
   It's about the **price I paid** trying to pull someone up who was never trying to rise in the
   first place.
   I met "Hugh" when I was 18.
   He was 30. Told me he was 28. (Let's call that **red flag #1** and move on.)
   We were together for 15 years. He went back and forth between me and another woman,
   had a child in the middle of it, and when she finally got tired and moved on—I thought I had
   won.

But I didn't win a prize.

I just got stuck holding the weight of a man who never truly saw my value.

We had a daughter—Sahara, my joy—and when she was nine months old, we got married.

Funny enough...

He proposed right after I made $27,000 in one month from real

estate.

Before that, his exact words to me were:

"It's going to be hard to close one of those deals."

Not, "You got this."

Not, "I believe in you."

Just a little sprinkle of doubt—*right before I proved him all the way wrong.*

At the time, I was working in property management. Rent was part of my compensation

package, so we lived rent-free. And even then—**he barely contributed financially.**

Not to the house. Barely to our daughter.

Hardly anything.

Then I saw a real estate listing: a two-bedroom, one-bath condo in Stockton for $85,000.

It was 2007. The market was shifting, but I knew real estate—and I saw potential.

I told him, "Let's go in on it together."

Getting his half of the down payment was like pulling teeth. He resisted, stalled, argued. But

eventually, we bought it.I handled the upgrades with my own money.

My parents painted it.

I used my real estate commission to redo the floors and counters.

Alberto, a contractor friend, gave me a deal on the work.

Hugh gave the **bare minimum**. Just enough to say he was "involved."

The rest was all me.

We rented it to a Section 8 tenant that I found. It broke even.

Not a dollar in profit—but it was holding.

Then came 2008.

The market crashed.

We were upside down.

I was offered a job in public transportation—**part-time**, lower pay, but it came with

benefits and a pension.

Hugh and I were already separated. I was raising Sahara on my own.

I moved back in with my parents to start over. She was enrolled in private school, and I was

paying $350/month for her tuition.

A few months later, I found a small one bedroom apartment in Oakland—$850/month. It

was a blessing. But every dollar I had was already spoken for.

Then my tenant moved out of the condo.

The panic I felt? *Unreal.*

I couldn't afford my rent AND a mortgage. I was barely hanging on.

Hugh and I were divorced by then.

He **fought hard** in court to get the condo—but the judge looked at him like:

"Sir... this property is upside down. There's no equity. There's nothing to split."

The judge even asked me if I could short-sale it. I said no. That would still destroy my
credit.

So the judge awarded it to me. Rightfully so. It was all in my name and we used my credit.

Out of desperation, I offered Hugh the chance to take it over.

"You want it? Fine. Take it. Just keep the payments up."

He said yes.

And that's when the *real* foolery began.

Late payments.

HOA violations.

Dogs he wasn't supposed to have. Too many people in the unit.Letters in my mailbox.

Calls to my phone.

My credit getting wrecked while he lived carefree.

I was calling, texting, trying to reason with him.

Nothing.

Then came *the* moment.

He stopped paying altogether.

I couldn't reach him.

I was done.

And then out of nowhere, he called me.

He had just gotten out of jail (don't ask), and he said, "I'm going to make the payment."

And I said, with *every ounce* of power I had:

"Keep your money. I don't want another dime from you. I'm done.

I'm not making one more payment on your behalf. Not to the bank.

Not to anyone. I'm done."

And I meant it.

I called the bank.
I let the foreclosure happen.
And I set myself free.
It hurt.
It messed up my credit for *seven years.*
But it saved my **mental health**, my **peace**, and my **future.**
Because keeping it would've meant staying in a cycle where I was begging for bare minimum
and paying with my sanity.
I started over.
Brick by brick.
From zero—again.
But this time, *without him.*

🔆 **Glow-Up Takeaway:**

●Don't let guilt or history tie you to dead weight.

●If someone didn't believe in you before the glow-up, they don't get to benefit from it.

●Love should never cost you your credit, your sanity, or your future.

●And sometimes, the *most powerful thing you can do...* is say:
"Keep your money. I'm done"

7

The Big Hustle Payoff

How I Built My Bag Slow, Strategic, and With Zero Handouts

Let's be real:

People love to romanticize the hustle.

But what they don't tell you is that the real payoff comes when you stop chasing quick

money—and start **building slow, quiet wealth that hits different.**

I started with a part-time public transportation job—working as a station agent, praying I'd

one day make it full-time.

And it took me *almost four years* to get there.

But when I did?

I started **moving different.**

Years earlier, I had read *The Automatic Millionaire by David Bach*, and that book rewired

something in me. It taught me the power of consistency—and

it stuck.

So the moment I had access to a retirement account, I started putting in $500 a month.

Even when I didn't have much. Even when life was chaotic.

$500. Every. Month.

And then I entered a supervisor training program at work—and that came with a *$15/hr*

raise. That's when I said:

"Max it out. Every paycheck. No matter what."

Because I knew—even if my real estate dreams took longer... even if the businesses didn't

pop off like I planned...

this retirement account was my safety net. My backup plan. My quiet

wealth-builder.

Now let's talk about reality:

I didn't get promoted right away.

I didn't stay in that program—I failed out on the *very last day.*

I was devastated.

But I didn't stop.I took another position as a transportation clerk. The job was less chaotic than being a

station agent (which had been traumatic, to say the least—I'd been assaulted, spit on,

drained mentally). But as a clerk, the money wasn't the same. The overtime disappeared. I had to adjust—**but I refused to stop maxing out my retirement.**

So what did I do?

I got my ass out there and *hustled.*

DoorDash.

Instacart.

Delivery runs.

Selling homes when I could through my real estate license.
Whatever it took.

I didn't care how tired I was—**I was not dropping the ball on my future.**

Even when I was short on bills, I made it work without pulling from that retirement

account.

I refused to break the system I was building.

Eventually, I bought a Honda Accord.

Paid it off with my tax return.

Kept grinding.

And then... **I got sick.**

Really sick.

I didn't know it at the time, but lupus was creeping in. My energy was disappearing. My

body was shutting down.

The man I was with left.

I spent five months bedridden.

But during that time—I wasn't done dreaming.

I started posting content online. I created *Latinas on Wall Street*—a brand that I later

realized was too narrow, but at the time, it gave me purpose. I was still trying to show the

world that I was okay, that I was still building something— even while I was falling apart

behind the screen.

Then came the **miracle**.

I applied for the supervisor role *again*—after being rejected *at least eight times* before.

I was done trying. I didn't believe they wanted me.But one day, I said something to my son's father about the position opening up again just a

few months after I was rejected yet again, and he looked at me and said:

"Are you gonna put in?"

I rolled my eyes.

"No. I already told you—they don't want me."

And he said something I will *never forget*:

"Then let *them* tell you no. You don't count yourself out."

I applied—just to prove a point.

And baby?

That was the time I got the job!

I was still so sick. Still weak. Still unsure if I could even show up. It was a struggle that

tested my will to survive.

But I forced myself out of bed and into that job.

And it. Changed. *Everything.*

The following year, I made over **$200,000**.

I stopped hustling for crumbs.

I stopped overexerting myself just to survive.

I didn't need side gigs anymore.

I had a *real income, a retirement plan, a pension*, and a foundation that would never leave

me broke again.

Now, after all the losses...

After the $50K mistake, the foreclosure, the heartbreak, the health crisis...

I have over $400,000 in my retirement account.

I'm building.

I'm still growing.

And I'm writing this damn book to tell you—

You don't have to get rich quick.

You just have to build smart, stay steady, and never count
yourself
out.

💡 **Glow-Up Takeaway:**
- Your day job isn't always a trap—it can be the launchpad.
- Building wealth quietly is just as powerful as building it publicly.
- Don't stop investing just because life gets hard—*that's when you need it most.*
- Max out the damn retirement account, sis. Your future self will thank you.
- And when they don't believe in you, ***apply anyway.***

8

Sis, Listen... (Advice to My Younger Self)

Because nobody told me—but I'm gonna tell you.

Sabrina, what I wish you knew is how valuable you are—*just as you are.*

Not for what you give. Not for how hard you try. Not for how much you prove.

You are worthy, even in your quietest, most unsure moments.

Because you are kind and nurturing, people will try to take advantage of you.

Not just in relationships.

The world will underpay you, overlook you, and expect more than it gives—especially if you're a woman.

They'll expect you to act smaller, softer, more accommodating.

But I need you to know: **you don't owe anyone your silence, your shine, or your struggle.**

And baby, you are not broken.

But you *do* need to heal.

You need to sit down with your truth—before it turns into trauma that runs the show.

That looks like therapy.

That looks like learning emotional intelligence.

That looks like listening to people wiser than you, even when you think you've got it figured out.

And please, hear me when I say this:

There is no shortcut to wealth.

No lottery ticket. No man. No magic trick.

If it came fast, it probably came with strings.

The only way to get there *and keep it?*

Hard work. Grit. Grind. And grace.

And the beautiful part?

You *can* do it.

You *will* do it.

One brick at a time.

You're going to build a home on a rock-solid foundation.

Even if that first brick is $5 a week.

Even if you don't make six figures.

Even if you're driving Uber or clocking in at FedEx.

You can start where you are—with what you have.

But the key?

Start.

Learn about compound interest.

Understand money.

Live below your means—not because you're broke, but because **you're wise.**

Retirement may feel a lifetime away.

But I promise you, if you start now...

By the time you're 50, you can look back and say: *"I did it."*

You won't need a man to save you.

34

You won't need to fake it for anyone.
You'll have **freedom**.
You'll have **peace**.
You'll have **receipts.**
And sweetie, I promise you with everything I've got—
I will *not* steer you wrong.

9

The Mindset Shift

From Looking Rich to Building Real Wealth

There's this moment—somewhere between your third financial heartbreak and your second overdraft fee—where it finally hits you:

"I don't want to look rich. I want to be free."

I wish I could tell you my mindset shift was this cute, glittery awakening.

You know—candles lit, sage burning, Beyoncé in the background.

But no, baby. Mine came in *silence*. In *humiliation*. In *mental and emotional exhaustion*.

I got tired.

Tired of the performance.

Tired of showing up looking polished when my account was screaming "Pending..."

Tired of chasing approval and possessions instead of peace.

At first, I didn't know what was happening.

I just started saying "no" a little more.

No to unnecessary spending.

No to emotional shopping.

No to trying to "keep up" with people who weren't even happy themselves.

I unfollowed people who made me feel behind.

I muted the noise that told me I needed more, better, faster.

And I started following **myself**.

Not the scared version. Not the broke version.

The *healed* version. The *disciplined* version. The *rich-in-the-making* version.

That's when the real glow-up started.

Because let's be honest: when you're living in survival mode, you *can't* shift your mindset.

You're just trying to keep the lights on.

But once I got even a little bit of breathing room?

I made a decision:

I don't care what it looks like. I care what it feels like.

And baby, it feels good to:

· Pay your bills early

·

· See your savings stack up

·

· Know your credit score is sexy

·

· Have **options**

·

Here's the truth I had to learn the hard way:

Looking rich is expensive.

Being financially free is priceless.
I stopped performing.
I started preparing.
And that shift? That quiet, steady, boring shift?
It changed everything.
Now I don't need a flashy bag to validate me.
I've got a portfolio.
I've got receipts.
I've got a damn plan.
And the best part?
You can start your shift at *any* moment.
All it takes is one decision.
One "no" that makes room for a bigger "yes."
So if you're reading this, and you're tired of the show—
Come sit with me.
Let's build the real glow-up.

✧ *Glow-Up Takeaway:*

The world will try to sell you the image of wealth.

But the real flex is freedom, peace of mind, and options.

Every dollar you keep, invest, or grow is a "yes" to your future self.

Start choosing the life you actually want to live—not the one you feel pressured to perform.

10

Budgeting for the Hot Mess

How to glow up your wallet without giving up everything you love

Let's get one thing straight—I didn't grow up knowing how to budget.

I didn't have a spreadsheet. I didn't read finance books at 18.

I was just trying to figure out how to stretch one paycheck across two weeks and a life I wanted *now*.

So if you're in the middle of a hot mess—emotionally, financially, or otherwise—this chapter is for you.

Because here's the one lesson that changed *everything* for me:

If you don't pay yourself first, you will never have money left over to save.

I know, I know—bills come first, right?

WRONG!

Here's what happens when you pay your bills first:

- The rent gets paid

- The car note clears
- The phone stays on
- You grab a bite here, a splurge there
- You tell yourself, "I'll save next check..."

And next check? Same story.

But when you flip the script and **pay yourself first**, something wild happens:

You start treating your savings like a *non-negotiable*.

Like rent.

Like lights.

Like oxygen.

Why it works:

When you pay yourself first—before the bills—you **create urgency.**

If you come up short on the light bill? You hustle.

If you're $80 short on rent? You figure it out.

You cut back, you drive Uber, you sell some clothes, you cancel subscriptions.

Because you *always find a way* to make sure everyone else gets paid.

So guess what?

It's time to put **you** on the damn payroll.

That $100? That $50? Even $10?

Slide it to your savings *before* the bills hit.

Suddenly, you're not "hoping" to save what's left—you're **saving first and letting the hustle fill in the rest.**

Real Talk:

If you don't build the habit now, when you have less—you won't magically start when you have more.

Because **money doesn't change your discipline. It magnifies it.**

So if your budget is a hot mess right now, here's where to start:

- Pick a percentage or a fixed number (ex: 10% or $100)
- Automate it to go straight to savings/investments
- Let the rest of your money deal with life
- Watch how creative, resourceful, and powerful you become

✧ Glow-Up Takeaway:

Pay yourself first, even when it feels impossible.
Because if you wait until it's easy, you'll be waiting forever.
You are not an afterthought.
You are the reason.
Budget like your future self depends on it—because she does.

11

You're Not Broke—You're Just Not Strategic Yet

The money isn't the problem. The plan is.

Let me lovingly say this right up front:

You're not stupid with money. You're just unpracticed.

You're not lazy. You're just overwhelmed.

You're not broke. You're just not strategic yet.

That was me—overworked, underpaid, doing the most, and still coming up short.

I was moving, hustling, showing up, checking all the boxes—and yet somehow the math still wasn't mathing.

It wasn't that I didn't have money.

It's that I didn't have a *strategy.*

Strategy > Struggle

We're taught to work hard.

But working hard **without direction** is how you end up tired, broke, and resentful.

You can't out-hustle a bad plan.

You can make $100,000 a year and still be broke if:

- Your bills eat your whole check
- You don't know where your money is going
- You save "when you can" instead of as a habit
- You're emotionally spending to escape your reality

That's not failure.

That's *financial survival mode.*

And the glow-up begins when you admit you're ready to stop surviving and start *strategizing.*

Here's what I had to learn the hard way:

1. **Money loves a mission.**
2. If your dollars don't have a job, they will disappear.
3. **Clarity is power.**
4. Know your income, know your bills, know your spending leaks.
5. **Discipline is freedom.**
6. The more focused you are now, the more freedom you'll have later.
7. **You don't need to be perfect—you just need a plan.**
8. Start with where you are. Track it. Adjust. Glow up.

43

I used to say, "I'm just not good with money."

No. That wasn't the truth.

The truth was that I never *learned* to be good with it.

No one taught me to budget.

No one showed me compound interest.

No one explained that wealth isn't about what you earn—it's about what you keep, invest, and grow.

So I stopped making excuses—and I started making a strategy.

I tracked my spending.

I created a bill calendar.

I automated my savings.

I paid myself first—even when it hurt.

I picked up extra shifts when I needed to, but I stopped leaning on hustle as the *only* plan.

Little by little, it added up.

And one day I looked at my accounts and realized: ***I'm not "trying" anymore. I'm doing it.***

✧ *Glow-Up Takeaway:*

You are not broke—you're just a strategy away from your breakthrough.

Stop calling yourself bad with money.

Start calling yourself *in progress.*

Make a plan. Work the plan. Adjust when needed.

You've got everything you need.

The glow-up is not waiting on money—it's waiting on *you.*

12

Your First $1K— Let's Get It

Because it's not about the number. It's about the power behind it.

Let's talk about your first thousand dollars.

Not the one you spent.

Not the one you borrowed and paid back.

Not the one that barely made it past payday.

The one you **kept**.

The one you **stacked**.

The one that **changed your whole mindset**.

There is something magical—spiritual, even—about that first $1,000 in savings.

Because it's not about the number.

It's about the fact that you did it.

You proved to yourself that you could be consistent.

You proved that you could hold onto money, not just make it.

And baby, let me tell you—I didn't start with a trust fund or a rich uncle.

I started with **$0** and a whole lot of **motivation**.
And that first stack?
It changed the way I saw myself.
I wasn't "trying to save."
I was a **saver**.

❀ Let's Break It Down: How to Stack Your First $1K

Whether you make $2,000 a month or $10,000—this works.

Step 1: Open a separate account

- Out of sight, out of mind
- No debit card attached
- Online-only banks work best for this
- Name the account something fun like **"Glow-Up Fund"** or **"Freedom Stack"**

Step 2: Set it, split it, forget it

- Pick your number: $25/week? $100/month? Whatever works—**commit and automate**
- Most employers let you split your **direct deposit** between two accounts
- Send your glow-up money straight to savings and the rest to checking
- If you never see it, you won't miss it
- *This is how savers are made.*

It's *all* your money—but after you pay your retirement and your glow-up fund, you'll spend what's left *without guilt.*

Step 3: Add your "surprise money"

- Birthday gifts
- Refund checks
- Rebates
- That random Venmo for watching someone's dog

Put it **ALL** in the pot. You'd be surprised how fast it adds up.

Step 4: Challenge yourself to a no-spend weekend or a hustle hour

- Sell something
- Drive a delivery shift
- Offer a service
- Cancel 1–2 subscriptions

Then drop that money in your stack.

Step 5: Watch what happens to your confidence.

- You'll start walking different.
- You'll start saying "Nah, I'm good" to dumb purchases.
- You'll stop confusing treating yourself with *cheating yourself.*

And when you hit that $1,000?

You'll know—you're not just dreaming about freedom.
You're **building** it.

✧ *Glow-Up Takeaway:*

Your first $1K isn't about being rich.

It's about proving to yourself that you are **powerful**, **consistent**, and **in control**.

It's the glow-up seed that becomes your emergency fund, your investment account, your launch pad.

You're not waiting for abundance—you're **stacking** it.

One direct deposit at a time.

And here's the truth they don't teach us:

$1,000 turns into $10,000. $10,000 becomes $100,000.

That's when the *real* glow-up begins.

When compound interest kicks in. When money starts working for *you*.

That's how freedom is built.

And it all starts with that first stack.

13

Emotional Spending Is Expensive

Buying peace is temporary. Building peace is forever.

Let's be real:

I didn't always spend money because I had it.

I spent money because I was tired.

Because I was lonely.

Because I wanted to feel in control of *something*.

Because I needed a quick hit of happiness.

Sometimes that $27 Target run was my therapy.

Sometimes I hit "add to cart" just to feel *seen*.

And yeah, sometimes I bought stuff I didn't need because I was trying to buy a feeling I couldn't name.

We don't talk about it enough, but this is what a lot of us go through:

We're not overspending because we're reckless.

We're overspending because we're *exhausted*.

The Cycle No One Talks About:

1. You're emotionally drained.
2. You want a quick lift.
3. You spend money on something that gives you a temporary high.
4. You feel guilt or shame later.
5. That emotional crash makes you want to spend again.

Rinse and repeat.

It doesn't mean you're broken.

It means you've been surviving—and spending became your self-soothing.

But let me tell you what nobody tells you:

Buying peace is temporary.
 Building peace is forever.
 That's what we're doing now—glow-up peace.
 The kind that doesn't come in a delivery box.
 The kind that comes from strategy, boundaries, and *self-worth.*

How to Break the Pattern:

1. Pause before you swipe.
 When you feel the urge to spend, stop and ask yourself:
 "What am I really trying to buy right now?"
 Validation? Control? Comfort?

2. Create a 'glow-up delay' list.

Anytime you want to buy something, write it down. Wait 48 hours.

Still want it? Cool.

Don't? Then you just saved your future self.

3. Replace the hit.

Find something else that brings dopamine *without draining your bank account*:

- A walk
- A call to a friend
- Journaling
- A podcast
- That playlist that makes you feel expensive

4. Celebrate a new kind of flex.

You know what feels better than an impulse buy?

Logging into your account and seeing that money still sitting there.

Peace is the new luxury.

✧Glow-Up Takeaway:

- You don't have to shame yourself for how you used to cope.
- You were doing the best you could.
- But now you're creating a life that doesn't need escaping.
- The new flex is *self-awareness*.
- The new luxury is *peace of mind*.
- The new glow-up is knowing you don't need to buy a vibe—

you *are* the vibe.

14

Stop Being The Family ATM

You can help without handing over your whole glow-up.

Let me say this clearly:
    Just because you love them
    doesn't mean you owe them your savings.
    Just because you made it out
    doesn't mean it's your job to pull everybody else up financially.
    Yes, you care. Yes, you're generous.
    But guess what?
    You're not the family's emergency fund.

Here's how it usually goes:

You get a raise.
    You start saving.
    You finally feel like you're catching your breath.
    And then—*ding*—a text.
    "Hey, can I borrow $200 real quick?"

"Can you help me pay my phone bill?"
"I'll pay you back Friday."
And the guilt kicks in.
You're doing okay, right? You should help, right?
But here's the truth:
Financial boundaries are part of the glow-up too.

Let's talk about why this happens:

- You're the responsible one
- You feel like if you say no, you're selfish
- You're scared of being seen as "bougie" or like you forgot where you came from
- You're trying to *fix* what other people never learned about money

But here's the kicker:
If you always bail people out, they never learn to swim.

🔆 *Glow-Up Rule:*

You can love people and still say no.
Boundaries don't mean you don't care.
They mean you care about yourself too.
You're allowed to say:

- "I'm not able to give, but I can help you brainstorm a solution."
- "I have a financial plan I'm sticking to right now."

· "No, I can't do that—but I love you."

And don't let people shame you for growing.

You sacrificed to get here. You *hustled* for this peace.

They weren't with you in the grocery store counting coins.

They weren't with you when your card got declined.

They weren't with you when you skipped meals to stretch your check.

So no—they don't get to swipe your glow-up card now.

✧Glow-Up Takeaway:

- You are *not* the family ATM.
- You are not a walking loan department.
- You are a whole-ass person with dreams, goals, and your own damn bills.
- You are allowed to protect your peace, your account, and your future.

And when you set boundaries, you don't just protect your bag— you teach your family what *true* financial empowerment looks like.

15

The Biggest Lie— "You Don't Make Enough to Save"

Sis. If you're earning money, you can start building wealth. Period.

Let me say this as clearly as possible:

You don't need a six-figure income to start saving.

You don't need a raise to start building.

You don't need "extra" money—you just need a plan.

The biggest lie we've ever been fed is:

"Once I make more money, I'll start saving."

No, you won't.

Because saving is a *habit*, not a dollar amount.

I've seen it all:

- People making $80K living check to check
- People making $35K with savings and peace of mind
- People making six figures and drowning in debt

- People with side hustles bringing in cash... and blowing every last dime

The truth?
  If you can't save $5, you won't save $50.
  And if you won't save $50, you won't save $500.

So let's flip the mindset:

It's not about how much you make.
  It's about what you *do* with what you have.
  Start small—but **start now**:

- $5 a week
- $10 from your tips
- That rebate check you forgot about
- The cash you didn't spend eating out

Even if it's just **one automatic deposit** every payday.
  That little stack builds the discipline that makes millionaires.

Your Glow-Up Math:
  Let's break this down real quick:
  $25 a week = $100 a month
  $100 a month = $1,200 a year
  $1,200 a year = **$12,000 in 10 years (not including interest)**
  And with compound interest?
  That number could double, triple, or more—just from showing up for yourself *consistently*.

But Here's the Hard Truth:

If you're spending more than you make, or if you don't know where your money's going every month...

No raise is going to fix that.

You don't need more money.

You need a *strategy* for the money you already have.

And once you master that?

Every raise, bonus, refund, and blessing becomes a tool—not a trap.

✧ **Glow-Up Takeaway:**

- You make enough to start.
- You just need to decide that your future is worth it.
- Stop waiting for "more."
- Start stacking with what you have.
- The glow-up doesn't wait for perfect conditions—it shows up for consistent effort.
- Let the world keep lying. You've got truth, tools, and a plan.

16

Your Glow-Up Budget Blueprint

Finally—a budget that doesn't feel like punishment.

If you've ever tried to follow one of those ultra-restrictive budgets that made you feel broke, bored, and trapped—you're not alone.

Most budgets fail because they forget one major thing:

You're a whole human being. Not a robot.

You're not going to stop living just because you're saving.

You're not going to cut out every joy in life to pay off debt.

And you don't need to.

You just need a **real-life glow-up plan** that works with your lifestyle and your goals.

So let's break down the Glow-Up Budget Method:

Step 1: Know your numbers. (Yes, all of them.)

- Before you can glow up your money, you've got to *face* your money.
- Log into those accounts.
- Pull up those bills.
- List out your income + your expenses.

Don't be scared. Be honest. This is your financial mirror—and it's where the change begins.

🔑 **Real Talk Check-In:**

If you've crunched the numbers and there's nothing left to save—*not even $5*—then this is your glow-up wake-up call:

It's not just a spending issue. It's an income issue.

That means it's time to **bring in more.**

Even if it's temporary. Even if it's exhausting.

A second job, a side hustle, selling something, freelancing—*whatever it takes* to bridge the gap.

You're not doing it forever.

You're doing it **so Future You can rest.**

The hustle up front = less stress later on.

This is *the season of planting.* The harvest comes next.

Step 2: Break it down into 4 categories:

Essentials (50%):
Rent, mortgage, utilities, groceries, car note—survival stuff.

Financial Goals (20%):
Savings, debt payments, retirement, investments

Lifestyle + Joy (20%):
Dining out, Netflix, nails, travel—yes, joy is part of the budget

Glow-Up Freedom (10%):
This is your "do what you want" money—guilt-free.
Blow it. Stack it. Save for Beyoncé tickets. Your choice.

Step 3: Pay yourself FIRST.

- That's right—*before* rent, *before* bills, *before* brunch.
- Automate your savings.
- Automate your investments.
- Make them non-negotiable.

If you pay yourself first, you'll figure out how to make the rest work.
If you pay yourself last, there will be nothing left.

Step 4: Use the envelope or bank account method
You don't have to carry cash (unless you want to), but separate your money:

- Bills Account

61

- Spending Account
- Savings Account
- Glow-Up Fund

Label them. Track them. Make it visual.
Put your money where your *intentions* are.

Step 5: Review weekly, adjust monthly.
This isn't set-it-and-forget-it.
Check in with your budget like it's a relationship.
"Am I still on track?"
"Where did I go over?"
"What worked for me?"
"What do I need to change?"
No shame. No drama. Just clarity.

✧Glow-Up Takeaway:

- A real glow-up budget gives you structure **and** freedom.
- It doesn't shame you—it *empowers* you.
- You're not budgeting to restrict your life.
- You're budgeting so you can build the life you *actually want*.
- This isn't about being perfect—it's about being **intentional**.
- The money glow-up starts with **alignment**, not anxiety.

17

The Truth About Credit— It's Not Your Enemy

Credit doesn't have to control you—you can control it.

Let me guess...

You were never taught how credit really works.

You just got handed a card, made some mistakes, and now you feel stuck.

But here's the truth:

Your credit score isn't a reflection of your worth.

It's just a number—and baby, numbers can be fixed.

Let's kill the shame first:

- You missed some payments?
- Maxed out a card?
- Co-signed and got burned?
- Got hit with collections?

Cool. Welcome to the club.

That's not the end of your story.

The glow-up doesn't care how you started—only that you start fixing it now.

The Credit Glow-Up Plan:

Step 1: Know where you stand.

You can't fix what you won't face.

Pull your credit report (free at annualcreditreport.com).

Look at all 3 bureaus: Experian, Equifax, TransUnion.

Check for:

- Errors (wrong addresses, accounts that aren't yours)
- Old collections that need resolving
- High balances dragging your score down

Step 2: Start cleaning it up.

Here's how you fix it—*not overnight, but over time:*

- **Make every single payment on time** (set reminders or auto-pay)
- **Keep your credit utilization under 30%** (If you have a $1,000 limit, don't carry more than $300)
- **Call creditors and negotiate payment plans or settlements**
- **Dispute errors directly with the bureaus** (you'd be shocked what gets removed)

And don't fall for credit repair scams—you can do *most* of this yourself.

Step 3: Start rebuilding.

Once your report is clean—or while it's in progress—start building new habits:

- Get a **secured credit card** (you put money down, they report your usage)
- Open a **credit-builder loan** through your bank or credit union
- Become an **authorized user** on someone's clean credit card (with their permission)
- Use your card for a small bill, pay it off monthly, and let time do its thing

This is a long game. Credit loves consistency.

Stop thinking credit is evil.

Credit is a *tool*—not a trap.

It's how people buy homes, build businesses, and create leverage.

The problem isn't the credit card.

It's not having a plan for how to use it.

When you glow up your credit, you glow up your *options*.

✧Glow-Up Takeaway:

- You are not your credit score.

- You *can* rebuild it. And you *will.*
- Stop avoiding the calls.
- Stop thinking it's too late.
- Stop saying "I'm just bad with money."
- Credit doesn't define your future—**you do**.

Now go get those points, baby. 🚀📊

18

Investing Isn't Just for Rich People

Stop watching other people build wealth. It's your turn.

Let me tell you what I used to think:

"Investing is for rich white men in suits."

"I'll start once I make more money."

"It's too complicated."

"I don't want to lose what little I have."

Sound familiar?

That's the lie.

That's the fear.

That's the gatekeeping—and it's been keeping too many of us broke for *too long.*

Here's the truth:

If you've ever bought a new iPhone, gone to brunch, or binged Netflix—you've *already helped someone else build wealth.*
 Now it's time to build your own.

Let's keep it simple: What is investing?

Investing is just putting your money somewhere it can *grow* over time.

- You're not spending it.
- You're not hiding it under your mattress.
- You're planting it. Watering it. Letting it multiply.
- Like a garden. With compound interest as your sunshine.

Where can you start?

1. Your Retirement Account (yes, that counts)

- 401(k), 403(b), TSP, or IRA
- This is investing. You're buying into funds that grow while you sleep.
- If your job offers a match? That's *free money.* TAKE IT.

2. A Roth IRA

- You put in post-tax dollars. It grows *tax-free.*

• That's right—tax-FREE withdrawals later. That's a gift.

3. Brokerage Accounts (like Fidelity, Vanguard, Charles Schwab)

- You can buy stocks, ETFs, or index funds
- You don't need thousands. You can start with $10.
- You don't need to "pick the winner." You can buy the *whole market* through index funds.

Quick Investing Glow-Up Rules:

💡 **Rule #1:** You don't need to be perfect. You just need to be *consistent.*

💡 **Rule #2:** Don't invest money you need tomorrow. This is a long game.

💡 **Rule #3:** Dollar-cost averaging is your bestie.

That means investing a set amount regularly—no matter what the market is doing.

💡 **Rule #4:** Index funds > trying to time the market

(They're low-cost, diversified, and beat most "experts" over time)

"But what if I lose money?"

You might. Temporarily.

But here's what people don't tell you:

The market always goes up—eventually.

Historically, it has always bounced back stronger.

What matters is time in the market, *not* timing the market.

Real Ones Know: Investing Is the Cheat Code

Rich people don't get rich from paychecks.

They get rich from *assets*—stocks, real estate, businesses that grow while they sleep.

And baby, you deserve that too.

✧**Glow-Up Takeaway:**

- You don't have to wait.
- You don't have to know it all.
- You just have to *start.*
- Start small.
- Start scared.
- Start with your future self in mind.

Because investing isn't just for rich people.

It's for *smart* people.

And you? You're one of them.

19

The Real Flex—Living Below Your Means

It's not about looking rich. It's about being free.

We've been sold the lie:

"If you look rich, people will *think* you're rich. And that's what matters."

But here's the truth:

Looking rich and *being* rich are two very different games.

And only one of them leads to peace, freedom, and *generational wealth.*

Let's get something straight:

Real flex? No car payment.

Real flex? Leaving a toxic job because you've got money stacked.

Real flex? Watching your investment account grow while

you're on vacation.

Real flex? Saying "I don't need that" and actually meaning it.

Living below your means isn't about deprivation.

It's about *delayed gratification*.

It's about choosing long-term freedom over short-term flex.

The mindset shift:

You don't have to prove anything to anyone.

You're not in a competition.

And nobody who truly has wealth is out here flashing it every day.

Quiet money is real money.

Loud money is often fake.

And what's loud today will be in collections tomorrow if you're not careful.

Here's what it looks like in real life:

- You could afford the designer bag—but you don't buy it.
- You upgrade your car *after* your net worth grows—not just when your paycheck does.
- You shop for deals, negotiate, and wait for sales—not because you're broke, but because you're *wise*.
- You don't cosign. You don't overspend. You don't flex for the 'Gram.

Because guess what?

Financial peace is louder than any status symbol.

You don't need a bigger check—you need a better plan.

If you're always spending up to the edge of your income, you'll always feel like you're barely getting by—even if you make six figures.

But when you live below your means?

You create space. Space to save. Space to invest. Space to breathe.

✧ **Glow-Up Takeaway:**

- Living below your means isn't a punishment—it's a *power move.*
- It's how you buy back your time.
- It's how you take back control.
- It's how you build real, unshakeable wealth.
- The glow-up isn't about impressing people.
- It's about *becoming* the version of you who doesn't have to.

And baby, that's the *real flex.*

20

The Paycheck Trap—Why You're Stuck (and How to Break Free)

You weren't lazy—you were just trying to survive.

Let's tell the truth that so many people are scared to say out loud:

Most people aren't "bad with money"—they're just stuck in a system that was never designed to help them win.

You're not a failure.

You're not behind.

You're just caught in a trap.

And until you name it, you can't change it.

What is the paycheck trap?

It's that loop where:

- You work hard...
- You get paid...
- You pay bills...
- You're broke again...
- And the cycle starts all over.

You never have enough to *get ahead*—because you're too busy trying to stay afloat.

Sound familiar?

This isn't laziness. It's burnout. It's survival mode.

And baby, you can't build an empire when your nervous system is fried.

The system counts on your exhaustion.

They sell you the dream of "financial freedom"—but they also sell you:

- 6-year car loans
- 30-year mortgages
- Credit cards for "emergencies"
- Student loans that'll follow you to the grave

They don't teach you how to build wealth.

They teach you how to stay a good little worker.

But not anymore.

75

Because *now* you know better. And when you know better? You do better.

How to break the trap:

1. Create a gap.
You have to earn more than you spend. Period.
Even if it means taking on a second hustle temporarily.

2. Pay yourself first.
Even if it's $10. Especially if it's $10.
Saving has to come before spending—or it won't come at all.

3. Start investing—even if it's small.
That's how you get out of the "work-for-every-dollar" grind.

4. Cut emotional spending.
Start asking:
"Am I buying this because I need it... or because I'm trying to feel better?"

5. Make a long game plan.
The trap only works if you don't have a map.
Set real goals. Track your progress. And glow the hell up with intention.

And let me be clear:

You don't have to quit your job to be free.

You just need your money to *work for you*—so your whole life doesn't depend on your next paycheck.

Freedom is when payday becomes a bonus, not a lifeline.

✧**Glow-Up Takeaway:**

If you've been living paycheck to paycheck, you are not broken.

You're just in a cycle that was never meant to empower you.

But guess what?

You're breaking it.

You're building something different.

And the life you're creating?

It won't depend on **luck**, **credit**, or a single damn employer.

That's not just a glow-up.

That's a *liberation.*

21

Rich vs. Wealthy—Know the Difference

Because one looks good. The other feels good.

Let's be real:

We've all been conditioned to chase the *look* of success.

Fancy cars. Designer bags. Luxury vacations.

That "I made it" aesthetic that makes people double tap.

But there's a difference between rich and wealthy—and baby, you better know it.

Here's the breakdown:

Being Rich = Having Money

But guess what? That money can be gone *tomorrow*.

Rich people often:

- Spend more than they earn
- Live paycheck to paycheck (just with bigger checks)

- Rely on appearances to prove success
- Have no long-term plan

Being Wealthy = Keeping Money + Making it Work for You
Wealthy people:

- Live below their means
- Invest consistently
- Let compound interest and time do the heavy lifting
- Don't need to prove anything to anyone

Wealth whispers. Rich screams.
And the ones screaming the loudest often have the least saved.
So the next time you feel like you're "behind" because someone else is flexing online—remember:
Wealth doesn't always photograph well.

Ask yourself:

- If your income stopped today, how long could you stay afloat?
- Do you own anything that's *growing* in value?
- Are you stacking for long-term freedom, or just living for short-term validation?

Let's go deeper:

Being wealthy isn't just financial.
  It's emotional. It's spiritual. It's physical.

- Do you sleep well at night knowing your bills are paid?
- Can you say no to people and protect your peace?
- Do you have freedom over your time, your energy, your choices?

That is wealth.
  And it's so much bigger than a dollar sign.

22

Be the Bank—How to Make Your Money Make Money

Wealthy people don't work harder. Their money works smarter.

Let's cut the fluff.
  You've been taught how to:

  · Work a job
  · Budget what you earn
  · Maybe save a little if there's anything left

But nobody ever taught you how to multiply your money.
  You wanna know what the wealthy have figured out?
  They don't just make money. They become the bank.

What does that even mean?

It means they lend.

They invest.

They own assets that produce cash flow—*not just consume it.*

They don't clock in for every dollar—they let their dollars go out and work shifts on their behalf.

And guess what?

You can do the same.

Here's how to "Be the Bank" in your own glow-up:

1. Earn Interest (Don't Just Pay It)

You've been paying interest on:

- Credit cards
- Car notes
- Loans

Time to flip that.

Open a high-yield savings account (HYSA) or CD (Certificate of Deposit) and let your cash *earn* something—even if it's just a few percent.

It's not life-changing money—but it's a shift in mindset:

"My money earns. I don't just spend."

2. Invest in Dividend-Paying Stocks & Index Funds

This is the sexy part.

Some investments pay you just for holding them.

- They're called *dividends*
- You get paid quarterly (or monthly)
- Reinvest them—and boom, you've got *compound interest stacking like magic*

Even better?

Many index funds (like VTI, SCHD, or SPY) pay dividends *plus* long-term growth.

That's double duty—passive income AND wealth-building.

3. Become a Lender, Not Just a Borrower

If you've ever borrowed money from a bank and paid it back with interest, congrats—you made someone else richer.

Let's flip it.

- You can use apps and platforms to invest in real estate loans (like Fundrise or Groundfloor)
- Or peer-to-peer lending if that fits your risk level
- And even offering private lending to someone you trust (carefully—with contracts!)

The game is: *don't just pay interest—* **collect it.**

4. Buy Assets That Pay You

This is the grown-money glow-up:

- A rental property
- A vending machine
- A digital product
- A course
- A planner

- A book

If it pays you in your sleep, it's an asset.
   If it drains your wallet every month, it's a liability.
   You're not chasing checks—you're building cash flow.

5. Leverage Like a Boss
   Banks use other people's money (OPM) all day long.
   So can you.
   Use credit the smart way:

- 0% intro APR cards for purchases you *already planned*
- Business credit to launch a side hustle
- Balance transfers to cut interest

But remember:
   Leverage is a tool—not a toy.
   Use it with a plan or don't use it at all.

✧Glow-Up Takeaway:

- You don't have to stay on the hamster wheel.
- You don't have to trade hours for dollars forever.
- You are not just a consumer.
- You are not just a spender.
- You are not just a worker.
- You are the damn bank now. 💳

And when your money starts earning, growing, and multiplying without you lifting a finger?

That's when the glow-up gets *generational.*

23

Your Financial Glow-Up Plan

Because knowledge is cute—but execution is
EVERYTHING.

You've made it to the end of this book.
    But don't get it twisted—this isn't the end of the journey.
    It's the beginning of your new one.
    The glow-up is real.
    And now you've got the tools to make it unstoppable.

Let's lock in the plan:

Step 1: Know your WHY.

If you don't know what you're building, you'll never stay
motivated to keep going.
    So ask yourself:

- What does freedom look like to me?

- Who am I doing this for—me, my kids, my future?
- What's the dream life I'm building, one dollar at a time?

Write that vision down. Tape it to your mirror. Speak it out loud.

Step 2: Track every dollar.

Not to punish yourself—but to *empower* yourself.
Every dollar is a soldier.
Tell it where to go.
Make it fight for your future.

- Use a budget (whatever kind works for you—digital, pen & paper, envelopes)
- Know your income, your expenses, your subscriptions
- Cut what doesn't serve you

Step 3: Pay Yourself First

You already know what it is. This rule never changes.
Before you give your money to bills, businesses, or brunch—
Set something aside for YOU.
Because freedom can't be built with leftovers.

Step 4: Automate your wealth

- Set your direct deposit to split into savings
- Auto-invest into your Roth or brokerage account
- Let your glow-up run on autopilot

If it's automatic, you don't have to rely on discipline.

Your systems will carry you even on the days you feel tired or scared.

Step 5: Keep learning

This book was your foundation. But don't stop here.

- Follow money creators.
- Take classes.
- Read books.
- Watch videos.
- Ask questions.
- Learn like your glow-up depends on it—because it does.

Step 6: Give yourself grace

You will mess up. You will fall off. You'll make dumb money moves sometimes.

But you're not starting over. You're starting *again*—with more knowledge.

Your glow-up isn't about perfection. It's about *progress*.

Step 7: Teach someone else.

Nothing will solidify your knowledge like sharing it.

· Teach your daughter how to save.
· Teach your brother how to budget.
· Teach your friend how to invest.

Because your glow-up?
It's *not just for you.*
It's for the whole community that's watching you rise.

✧ **Glow-Up Takeaway:**

This isn't a fairytale.
This isn't a pipe dream.
This isn't a "maybe someday."
This is YOUR time.
Right here.
Right now.
You've got a plan.
You've got receipts.
You've got a story that can't be denied.
And best believe—you've got the power to change your entire financial destiny.
So go get your freedom.
Go get your peace.
Go get your bag.
Go get your **LIFE.**

Your glow-up is already happening.
Now go *live it out loud.* 🖤🫶💥

About the Author

Sabrina Colón is a powerhouse leader, mother, survivor, and transformational speaker whose voice has been shaped by faith, grit, and a glow-up that came from the inside out.

A transportation supervisor by trade and a healer by spirit, Sabrina has turned personal pain into purpose—now using her story to empower women to rise, rebuild, and reclaim their power.

From Rock Bottom to Rich Energy is her debut book, and a comeback anthem for women who've ever felt broke, broken, or overlooked.

Sabrina writes, speaks, and leads with the belief that late bloomers still blossom, and divine timing is always on time.

She lives in the Bay Area with her children, her dreams, and her deep belief in what's next.

To connect or book Sabrina for your next event, follow **@itssabrinacolon** on Instagram, visit **SabrinaSpeaks.com** for more.

You can connect with me on:

- https://sabrinaspeaks.com
- https://facebook.com/sabrinacolon
- https://instagram.com/itssabrinacolon

www.ingramcontent.com/pod-product-compliance
Lightning Source LLC
Chambersburg PA
CBHW031221120626
46545CB00003B/941